ELEPHANT MAN

Title of the original Norwegian edition: *Elefantmannen*
© 2013 Cappelen Damm
English translation © 2015 Rosie Hedger

Annick Press Ltd.

Cataloging in Publication

Di Fiore, Mariangela
[Elefantmannen. English]
    Elephant man / Mariangela Di Fiore ; illustrated by Hilde Hodnefjeld ; translated by Rosie Hedger.

Translation of: Elefantmannen.
Issued in print and electronic formats.
ISBN 978-1-55451-778-7 (bound).—ISBN 978-1-55451-779-4 (html).—
ISBN 978-1-55451-780-0 (pdf)

    1. Merrick, Joseph Carey, 1862–1890—Juvenile fiction.
I. Hodnefjeld, Hilde, illustrator II. Title. III. Title: Elefantmannen. English

PZ7.D488El 2015   j839.823'8   C2015-900752-6
                                          C2015-900753-4

Published in the U.S.A. by Annick Press (U.S.) Ltd.

Printed in China

Visit us at: www.annickpress.com

Also available in e-book format. Please visit www.annickpress.com/ebooks.html for more details. Or scan

Elephant Man

Mariangela Di Fiore

Illustrated by

Hilde Hodnefjeld

translated by Rosie Hedger

annick press
toronto + new york + vancouver

"Gather round—prepare to be amazed! I promise you that you've never before seen the likes of this. A sight so disgusting, so very gruesome, that you simply won't believe it until you see it with your own eyes.

"Ladies and gentlemen! It is my honor to introduce ... **the Elephant Man!**"

Every evening the Elephant Man, whose real name is Joseph Merrick, is the main attraction at a tiny little theater on Whitechapel Road in London. People swarm to this theater to see strange folks of every description. They cry out in dismay at the sights on display: a bearded woman, tiny dwarfs, contortionists, and a man so very thin that he looks like a walking skeleton.

Their screams are most piercing when Joseph steps on stage.

Joseph sighs as he gazes upon his audience.

He doesn't like to see them scream in terror as they catch sight of him. He'd much rather bring happiness and laughter to others. Above all, he'd love to laugh with them.

Joseph hadn't always looked this way. When he was born, he looked like any other baby. His mother held him close and thought he was the most beautiful child she had ever seen. But when Joseph was only a few years old, something unusual happened to him. He started to smell unpleasant, and large, crumpled lumps that looked like cauliflowers began to grow all over his body. These lumps made his mouth feel heavy and change shape, and it became difficult for him to speak properly. He lost the ability to smile and could no longer make different facial expressions. His feet and one hand grew swollen, his head became unnaturally large, and from his forehead grew what looked like the start of a trunk.

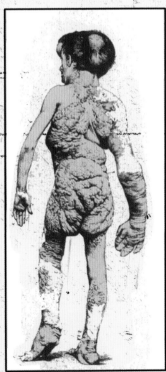

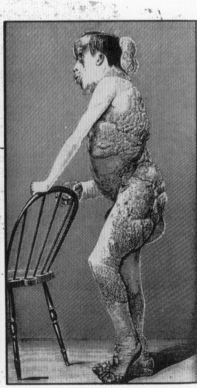

When Joseph was 11 years old, his mother died. Joseph was devastated. He cried and cried as if his tears might never stop. Joseph's father was also upset, but it wasn't long before he remarried. Joseph's stepmother was not remotely pleasant, and every evening Joseph was forced to go to bed on an empty stomach. "An ugly boy like you doesn't deserve a scrap to eat!" she would tell him.

Joseph was only 12 years old when his stepmother decided that he must leave school and start work, but it wasn't easy for Joseph to find a job. His body grew more deformed with each passing day, and nobody wanted to hire anybody who looked the way he did.

Eventually Joseph found a job in a cigar factory. He was so proud that he practically trembled with delight on his first day at work.

"Hello, I'm Joseph and I can't wait to work with you all!" he announced, using his very best manners to greet his new workmates. They stared back at him, aghast. "Who on earth is that ugly, smelly creature? He can't even speak properly!" he heard them whisper.

Joseph was dismayed. He felt like running away from everything and everyone, but he put on a brave face. *It won't be long before things get better*, he thought. *They just have to get to know me, that's all.*

But the whispering continued. None of the others wanted to sit next to Joseph while they worked, and even during breaks he was forced to sit by himself each and every day. "Just looking at him puts me off my lunch!" he heard a worker comment.

Joseph tried to pretend nothing was wrong, forcing back tears and working all the harder. But it wasn't long before he had dropped a whole tray of cigars, accidentally scattering them across the factory floor. The others shook their heads in resignation. "You had better pull yourself together," they grumbled loudly. This was not the first time Joseph had dropped things at work. "Lumbering oaf!" shouted another. "Lazybones!"

But Joseph was not lazy. It wasn't at all easy for him to work with his swollen hand, and his arm had grown too heavy for him to lift.

"They should send him packing!" one of Joseph's workmates mumbled as they watched him pick up the cigars he had dropped. Joseph felt something warm running down his cheek.

Joseph lost his job at the cigar factory. Night after night he lay awake worrying. How would he earn a living now? One day he tried his hand at street trading. He wore a long overcoat, hiding his face behind a large hood. He made a small hole he could see through and topped off his outfit with a wide-brimmed hat. All the same, when Joseph reached out to pass people the items they had purchased, they would flee at the sight of his deformed hand. Most people avoided coming anywhere near him because he smelled odd, and even the stray dogs roaming the streets kept their distance.

At home things grew worse and worse. Joseph's stepmother was often angry. She screamed and shouted at Joseph and accused him of exploiting the goodwill of his family, even though he spent hours every day looking for a job. On many occasions Joseph didn't even dare to go home for dinner. His stomach rumbled and he grew dizzy with hunger, but he still preferred to wander alone through the streets rather than face his stepmother. One day Joseph's stepmother forced his father to make a decision: "Either he goes, or I do!" she declared.

Tom Norman

The streets of London were bitterly cold. A thick fog shrouded them as rats scurried along the gutters. Joseph couldn't help but shiver. He had neither money nor a place to live. He knocked at the doors of all the factories and shops in the city to ask if anyone might consider employing him, but people simply shook their heads.

Joseph saw no other option than to accept an offer from Tom Norman, a showman and manager of a small theater company.

Tom Norman was convinced that he could make a lot of money by putting Joseph on stage. "People love to see ugly things on display," he explained to Joseph, and he was right. Every evening long lines of people paid to come and peer at Joseph.

But even though Joseph had a job, he wasn't at all happy. He missed having friends who would care for him. He longed to spend time with people with whom he could laugh and talk. He loved reading books, and his imagination was overflowing with fantastic tales. He often wrote beautiful poems and stories in which people were kind to one another and understood that you could be a good person even if you weren't very good-looking. In his stories, no one was judged by his appearance. But what use was it having all these tales to tell without anyone to share them with? In his dreams Joseph had friends he could delight with his marvelous stories; they would read books to one another, share jokes, and discuss art and music.

But every time Joseph woke up, he found himself as alone as ever.

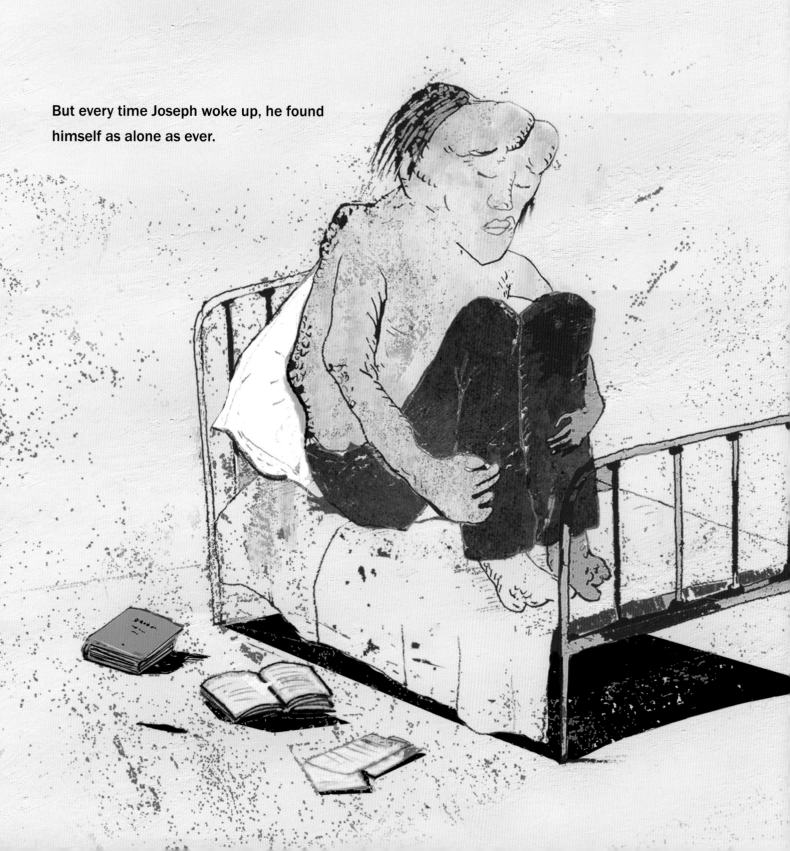

One day a doctor stopped by the theater. His name was Frederick Treves and he had heard rumors about Joseph and his disfigured body. He asked if Joseph would join him on a trip to the London Hospital for an examination. Joseph and Frederick spent a whole day together at the hospital.

It was the best day Joseph had ever known! Even though Joseph's speech could be difficult to understand, Frederick followed everything he had to say. He talked to Joseph about ordinary things, asking questions and taking an interest in his life. He treated Joseph like a human being rather than a monster.

When Frederick accompanied Joseph back to the theater that evening, he gave him a card printed with his name and address. "I hope that we might meet again," he said. Joseph felt a warm glow of happiness. There was nothing he would like better than to spend more time with Frederick. Joseph wished he were able to smile at him to show just how happy and grateful he felt, but it was as if Frederick understood all the same. "Then we'll meet again," he said, giving Joseph a friendly pat on the shoulder. Joseph felt like a new man. Finally he had made a friend! All he wanted now was to meet with Frederick again as soon as possible. However, Tom Norman had other plans for Joseph.

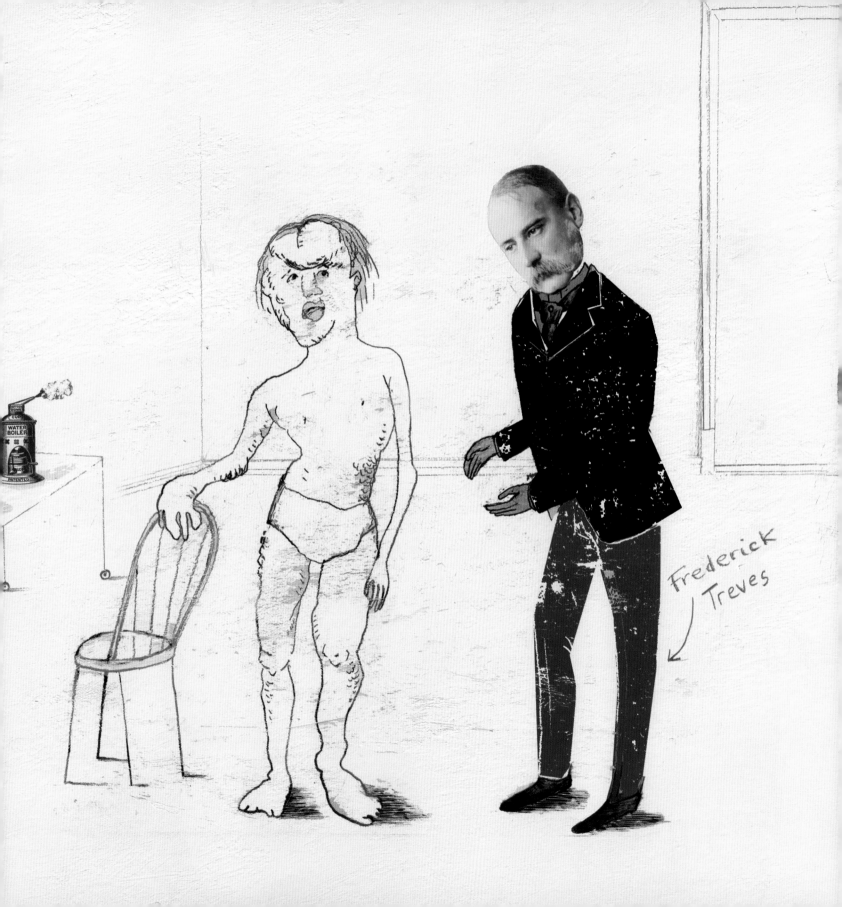

Frederick
Treves

"You're going on tour!"

Joseph was to be sent around Europe, where he would be put on show in many different countries. Tom Norman told him that a man from Austria would be accompanying him throughout his tour, and he had promised Joseph money and fame. "You're going to be rich!" Tom assured him.

Well, I suppose it might be nice to travel a little and to see different countries, Joseph said to himself.

But Joseph couldn't see much more than a narrow strip of light and billowing clouds of dust through the tiny crack in the carriage that transported him from city to city. The Austrian was grumpy and scolded Joseph no matter what he said or did. As they traveled through country after country, Joseph sat forlorn in the dark carriage. He daydreamed about green fields, bubbling brooks, and the lapping of waves against the shore. He imagined sitting in the shade of a tree and hearing the breeze as it rustled the treetops. *Maybe I can use the money I earn to take a trip to a beautiful place*, Joseph thought. Tom Norman had been right about one thing: Joseph had earned a lot of money on his tour.

In all of the cities he visited, people flocked to see him, and each of them paid handsomely. Every evening the Austrian took the money Joseph earned and placed it in a small box.

"I'll look after this so you don't lose it," he explained to Joseph.

One morning Joseph awoke in Belgium to discover that he was alone in the carriage.

The Austrian had vanished, and with him all the money Joseph had earned. Joseph waited all day for the Austrian to return. Perhaps he'd popped out to buy them some food? Or some new clothes? Joseph looked down at his ragged attire.

Joseph waited and waited. He grew more afraid with every passing moment. He was all alone in a foreign land. He had no money and he didn't understand the language. Eventually he realized that the Austrian had no plans to return. Joseph sat inside the carriage, his arms wrapped protectively around himself. His whole body shook. What was he going to do? Where would he go?

Joseph plucked up his courage. He pulled on his coat, hood, and hat and stepped out of the carriage. The sunlight was bright and Joseph squinted as he nervously observed his surroundings. There were strange buildings everywhere. He tried to ask people for help to find his way home, but they all spoke a language he didn't understand.

For a while he stood, gazing around in confusion. Then he started to make his way through the streets. People pointed and stared at him, but he ignored them. As he passed a pawnbroker's shop, he had an idea. He hurried into the shop, rifled through his pockets for any items of value, and placed everything he found on the pawnbroker's counter. The pawnbroker stared at him suspiciously before taking a closer look at what Joseph had pulled from his pockets. He mumbled something Joseph didn't understand before handing him some coins.

The visit to the pawnbroker's shop had brightened Joseph's day. The coins jingled in his pocket. Now he just had to find a way to return to England. Joseph walked and walked. His feet grew sore and his stomach rumbled with hunger. Eventually he made it to the railway station! He bought a ticket and had barely sat down before he nodded off, completely exhausted.

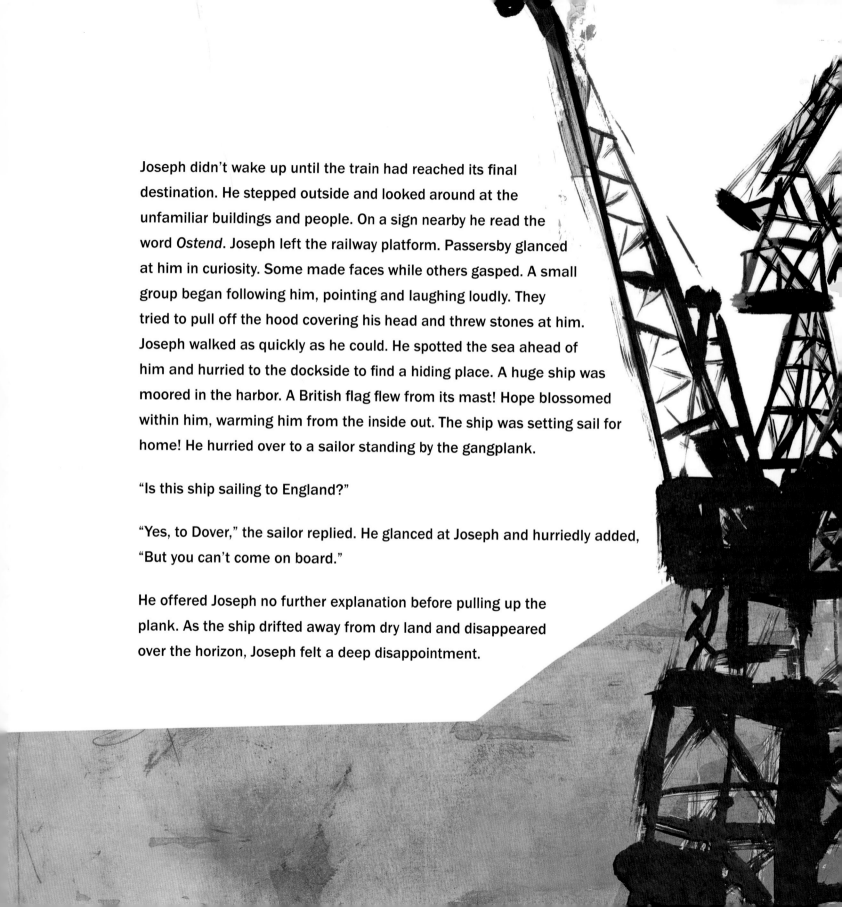

Joseph didn't wake up until the train had reached its final destination. He stepped outside and looked around at the unfamiliar buildings and people. On a sign nearby he read the word *Ostend*. Joseph left the railway platform. Passersby glanced at him in curiosity. Some made faces while others gasped. A small group began following him, pointing and laughing loudly. They tried to pull off the hood covering his head and threw stones at him. Joseph walked as quickly as he could. He spotted the sea ahead of him and hurried to the dockside to find a hiding place. A huge ship was moored in the harbor. A British flag flew from its mast! Hope blossomed within him, warming him from the inside out. The ship was setting sail for home! He hurried over to a sailor standing by the gangplank.

"Is this ship sailing to England?"

"Yes, to Dover," the sailor replied. He glanced at Joseph and hurriedly added, "But you can't come on board."

He offered Joseph no further explanation before pulling up the plank. As the ship drifted away from dry land and disappeared over the horizon, Joseph felt a deep disappointment.

Suddenly Joseph heard a voice. A man was at his side speaking in perfect English. "I'm sorry. I overheard that gentleman say he wouldn't allow you on board. Are you trying to get to England?" he asked in a friendly manner.

Joseph nodded. "Yes, I do so want to get home to England. Can you help me?" he asked, hopeful.

"Yes, I know a way," the man replied, offering Joseph an outstretched hand. "My name is Wardell Cardew, by the way. I'm English too."

With Wardell Cardew's help, Joseph made it to Antwerp, and following Cardew's directions he found the city port. There he spotted another ship flying the British flag. He could take it instead! Having been rejected once before, Joseph didn't dare ask for permission this time. He stole on board and hid in the cargo hold.

Joseph lay there all night long. He was regularly soaked through by icy sprays of seawater and he shivered with cold. To make matters worse, he felt terribly seasick and vomited several times. The thought of being back in England before long gave him the strength he needed to last the journey.

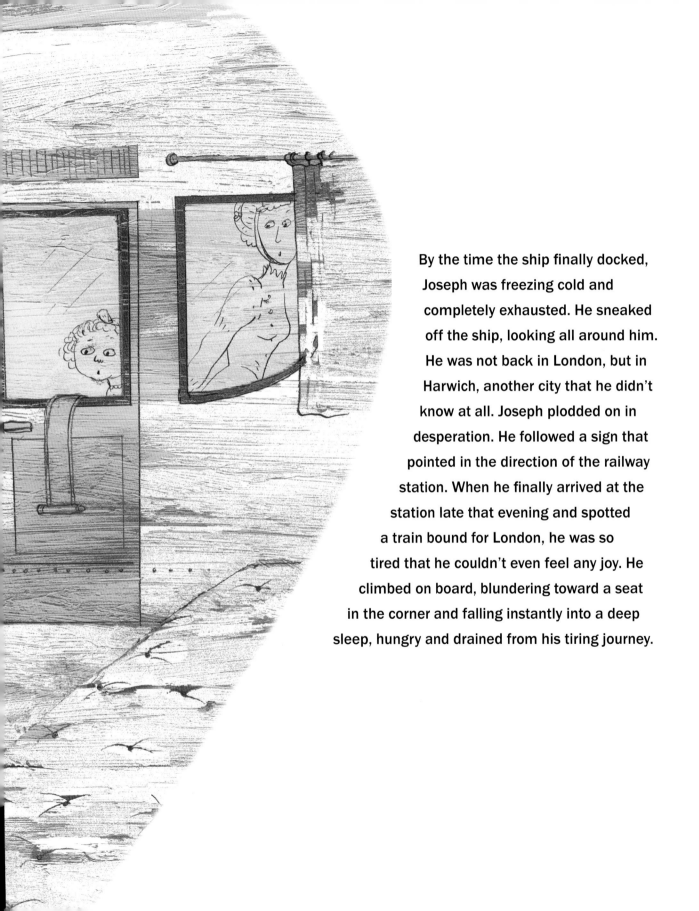

By the time the ship finally docked, Joseph was freezing cold and completely exhausted. He sneaked off the ship, looking all around him. He was not back in London, but in Harwich, another city that he didn't know at all. Joseph plodded on in desperation. He followed a sign that pointed in the direction of the railway station. When he finally arrived at the station late that evening and spotted a train bound for London, he was so tired that he couldn't even feel any joy. He climbed on board, blundering toward a seat in the corner and falling instantly into a deep sleep, hungry and drained from his tiring journey.

The following morning Joseph was woken by loud screams. He jumped, rubbing his eyes. All around him stood a ring of passengers, looking aghast. His hood had slipped off during the night. He hurriedly pulled it back into place, hiding his face from the crowd.

"Call the police, there's a monster on board!" cried one of the passengers.

F. Treves
London Hospital

Even the policemen paled at the sight of Joseph. "Who are you? Where do you come from?" they asked. Joseph told them about the tour and the Austrian who had disappeared with his money.

"Don't you have a family you can turn to?" the police inspector asked him. Joseph explained that his mother was dead and his father wanted nothing to do with him.

"Is there nobody we can contact?"

Joseph shook his head sadly. The policemen looked at each other, puzzled. "What are we going to do with him?" they whispered. "We'll need you to empty your pockets to see if we can find any clues about your identity," one of the policemen told him.

Joseph pulled out the card that the doctor, Frederick, had given him on the day they spent at the hospital.

"Do you know Frederick Treves?"

Joseph nodded proudly. The policemen took Joseph down to the station and called Frederick.

It didn't take long for Frederick to arrive and collect Joseph. "Do you want to come with me to the London Hospital? We can arrange a pleasant room for you to live in," he said. Frederick's offer warmed Joseph's heart. Of course he wanted to go with Frederick! He was famished and weary and covered head to toe in dust and dirt after his long journey. When they reached the hospital, Frederick made sure that Joseph could take a bath, change into some clean clothes, and enjoy a delicious meal.

Joseph was happy at the London Hospital. He had his own room in which he always felt safe. Nobody shrieked and wailed when they saw him and nobody bullied him. He spent time with Frederick every day. They would talk for hours, and while Frederick studied Joseph's crumpled skin and the lumps on his body, Joseph recited his poetry and told him some of the stories he had written. Frederick lent Joseph piles of books, and whenever Joseph finished reading one, he and Frederick would discuss it together. Occasionally Frederick brought medical students to Joseph's room. Joseph had to stand naked before them as they took notes, pointed, and discussed things with one another. Joseph didn't like it very much; he felt stupid and ugly in front of them. Even so, the students were kind—they didn't cry out in fear or laugh at him.

When Joseph wasn't reading or writing he liked to make things. He had a model kit for a marvelous cathedral made of cardboard, and he constructed it eagerly. It took a long time to build with his lumpy, heavy hand, which didn't always do what he wanted it to. Nonetheless, Joseph was patient. He felt such delight at seeing his cardboard cathedral take shape. It was so wonderful to make things!

On Joseph's mantelpiece stood a small painting of his mother. Several times every day Joseph would look at the painting and be reminded of her, and how kind and beautiful she had been. He thought it was strange that he could have ended up with such a horrible outward appearance when his mother had been so beautiful. He mentioned this to Frederick one day as they admired the painting together. "But you're beautiful inside, Joseph," Frederick replied reassuringly.

Frederick tried to encourage Joseph to go out once in a while. "You need a little fresh air, and it will be good for you to meet new people," he said. But Joseph didn't dare. He couldn't even face the prospect of taking a walk in the hospital gardens. Sometimes he would sit at his open window and listen to the birdsong and wind whistling through the treetops. He longed to be outside, but he was afraid of meeting people who might squeal in fright when they caught sight of him. Inside his room he felt safe and sound.

Frederick devised a plan. He called his good friend Leila Maturin and asked if she would like to meet Joseph.

Joseph was enchanted when Leila Maturin unexpectedly entered his room. She was beautiful, elegant, and fragrant with the scent of a wonderful perfume.

She approached Joseph, taking his hand and greeting him as a friend. Joseph began to cry. He cradled his head in his hands and sobbed. Neither Leila nor Frederick understood.

"Don't you think it's nice to have a visitor?" Frederick asked, surprised by Joseph's reaction.

"I do," Joseph replied. "I'm crying because I'm so happy. Never since my mother died has a woman smiled at me."

Joseph made several friends. Many rich, well-known people from London's high society heard about Joseph and came to visit. They admired his cardboard cathedral and listened to his stories. He talked with his guests for hours at a time about books, art, and theater.

One day a surprise visitor took Joseph's breath away. Princess Alexandra of Wales knocked at his door. She had also heard about Joseph and was keen to meet him.

"I've heard that you like reading and writing poetry," the princess said. "Would you be so kind as to read a poem to me?"

In a timid voice, Joseph read his favorite poem.

'Tis true my form is something odd
But blaming me is blaming God
Could I create myself anew
I would not fail in pleasing you

If I could reach from pole to pole
Or grasp the ocean with a span
I would be measured by the soul
The mind's the standard of the man

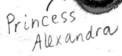

'Tis true my form is something odd,
But blaming me is blaming God;
Could I create myself anew
I would not fail in pleasing you.

If I could reach from pole to pole
Or grasp the ocean with a span,
I would be measured by the soul;
The mind's the standard of the man.

By Joseph Merrick, with lines
borrowed from a poem by
Isaac Watts

Princess
Alexandra

One day Frederick had something important to tell Joseph. "You have a very rare disease. It makes you disfigured on the outside, but inside you are like anyone else. We knew that already, of course," Frederick said, giving Joseph a kindhearted smile.

A wave of relief flooded over Joseph. Finally, he understood the reason he looked the way he did. He was not an elephant. He was a person! A person with an illness! He was not a monster or a beast, as so many people had told him.

That day, Joseph plucked up the courage to venture out into the garden behind the hospital. The grass was wet with dew and the sun radiated lovely, warm rays of light that made everything shine. Joseph stood where he was, captivated, gazing at all that surrounded him. The boughs of the trees swayed in the breeze and the sparkling sunlight dappled the green leaves. The bees collected pollen from the flowers, buzzing gently on their way, and a butterfly fluttered by, its wings beautiful and bright. Joseph took a deep breath. He removed the large coat that he so often hid within and pulled off his hood, throwing it far, far away.

This is what researchers think Joseph would have looked like if he hadn't had his illness

PHOTO RECONSTRUCTION (TOP RIGHT) BY JUDE MARIS

AFTERWORD

Joseph Merrick continued to live at the Royal London Hospital until his death on April 11, 1890. He was 27 years old.

The official cause of his death was suffocation, but Frederick Treves carried out an examination of Joseph's body and believed that he died from a dislocated neck. Due to the weight of his large head, Joseph was forced to sleep sitting up, but Treves thought that Joseph may have tried to fall asleep lying down in an attempt "to be like everyone else."

Medical experts still aren't sure exactly what caused Joseph's deformities. The latest research suggests he suffered from Proteus syndrome (a genetic condition that makes skin, bones, and muscle tissue grow abnormally), possibly combined with a disease called neurofibromatosis type I. Both are caused by genetic mutations that would have happened before Joseph was born.

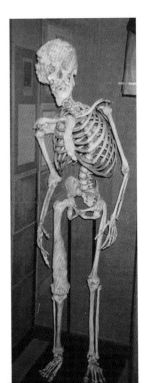

Joseph Merrick's skeleton is held in a glass cabinet at the Royal London Hospital, where it can be viewed by doctors and medical students. Joseph's cardboard cathedral is on display at the hospital's museum.

There are various accounts of Joseph Merrick's life from people who knew him. While this story is based on those accounts, the author has used her imagination to recreate Joseph's thoughts and conversations.

Joseph Merrick
London Hospital

Joseph, as he looked a few months before he died

Miss L Mat...
Sunderlan...
Isla...

West Coast of Scotland

Joseph's specially built armchair

Joseph's skull

Dear Miss Maturin

Many thanks indeed for my grouse, and book, you so kindly sent me, the grouse were splendid I saw Mr Freres on Sunday He said I was to give his best respects to you With much Gratitude. I am Yours Truly

Joseph Merrick
London Hospital
Whitechapel

The only known example of Joseph's letter-writing, to Mrs. Leila Maturin

Joseph in his finest attire, around 1889, the year before he died

Joseph's hat and hood

MORE ABOUT JOSEPH MERRICK

BOOKS

Howell, Michael, and Peter Ford. *The True History of the Elephant Man: The Definitive Account of the Tragic and Extraordinary Life of Joseph Carey Merrick.* New York: Skyhorse, 2010.

Montagu, Ashley. *The Elephant Man: A Study in Human Dignity*. Lafayette, LA: Acadian House, 2001. First edition 1971.

Treves, Sir Frederick. *The Elephant Man and Other Reminiscences*. London: Cassell and Company, 1923. Open Library, 2008. openlibrary.org/books/OL6660332M/ The_elephant_man_and_other_reminiscences.

Vicary, Tim. *The Elephant Man*. Oxford: Oxford University Press, 2006.

FILM

The Elephant Man. Directed by David Lynch. Released 1980. Hollywood: Paramount Home Video, 2003. (DVD, 124 minutes.)

WEBSITES

Joseph Carey Merrick Tribute Website. jsitton.pwp.blueyonder.co.uk/elephantman/ elephant_man.htm.

Pednaud, J. Tithonus. "Joseph Merrick—The Elephant Man." The Human Marvels website, 2008. thehumanmarvels.com/joseph-merrick-the-elephant-man.

Mariangela Di Fiore has an Italian father and a Norwegian mother and lives in Norway. She studied literature at the University of Oslo and screenwriting at the University of California in Los Angeles. Her previous publications include a number of books for young people, a cookbook, and a nonfiction book and accompanying documentary for adults on the mafia organization Camorra.

Hilde Hodnefjeld is a Norwegian illustrator, trained at the Oslo National Academy of Arts. She has also studied in Paris and in Iceland. She works as an illustrator and graphic designer. In 2011 she was nominated for the Norwegian Ministry of Culture Illustration Prize for illustrating the book *The Master of Farting*.

Rosie Hedger was born in Scotland and completed her MA in Scandinavian Studies at the University of Edinburgh. She lived and worked in Norway, Sweden, and Denmark before returning to the United Kingdom, where she works as a literary translator from Norwegian.